M000215670

The Good Citizen's Alphabet

BERTRAND

DRAWINGS BY FRANCISZKA THEMERSON

RUSSELL

THE GOOD CITIZEN'S ALPHABET

 HISTORY OF THE WORLD
in epitome

TATE PUBLISHING

THE GOOD CITIZEN'S ALPHABET

This book, it is felt, will supply
a lacuna which has long disgraced
our educational system. Those who
have had the largest amount of

experience in the earlier stages of
the pedagogical process have in a
very large number of cases been
compelled to conclude that much
unnecessary difficulty and much
avoidable expenditure of school
hours is due to the fact that the
ABC, that gateway to all wisdom, is
not made sufficiently attractive to
the immature minds whom it is
our misfortune to have to address.
This book, small as is its compass,
and humble as are its aims, is, we
believe and hope, precisely such
as in the present perilous conjuncture

is needed for the guidance of the first steps of the infant mind. We say this not without the support of empirical evidence. We have tried our alphabet upon many subjects : Some have thought it wise ; some, foolish. Some have thought it right-minded ; others may have been inclined to think it subversive. But all — and we say this with the most complete and absolute confidence — all to whom we have shown this book have ever after had an impeccable knowledge of the alphabet. On this ground we feel convinced that our education authorities, from the very first moment that this work is brought to their attention, will order it instantly to be adopted in all those scholastic institutions in which the first elements of literacy are inculcated.

17th January 1953   *B.R.*

A

Asinine

—What *you* think.

B

Bolshevik

—Anyone whose opinions I disagree with.

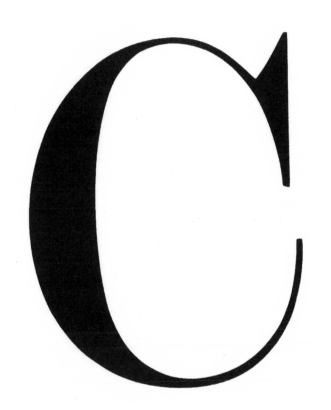

Christian

—Contrary to the Gospels.

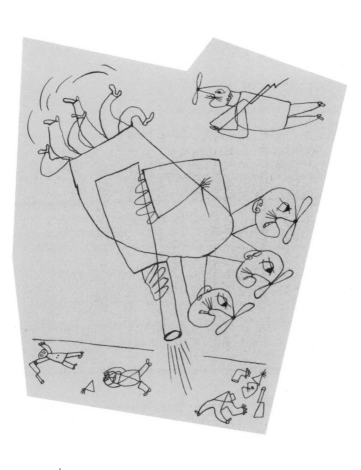

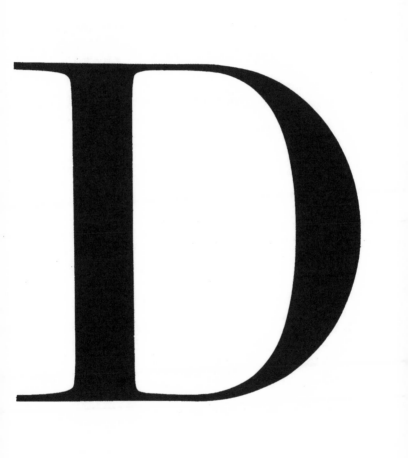

Diabolic

—Liable to diminish the income of the rich.

Erroneous

—Capable of being proved true.

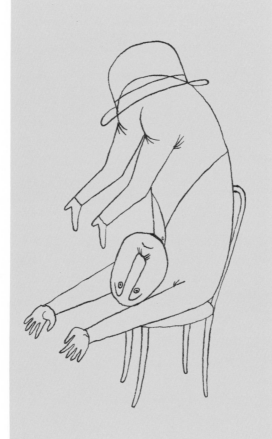

Foolish

—Disliked by the police.

Greedy

—Wanting something I have
and you haven't.

H

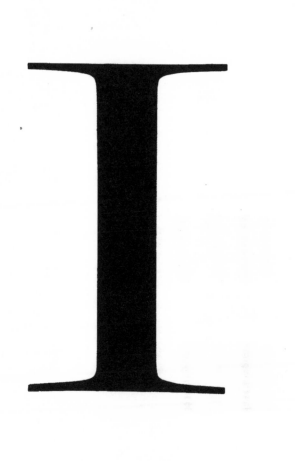

Holy

—Maintained by fools for centuries.

Ignorant

—Not holy.

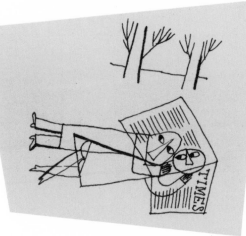

Jolly

—The downfall of our enemies.

K

Knowledge

—What Archbishops do not doubt.

Liberty

—The right to obey the police.

M

Mystery

—What I understand and you don't.

Nincompoop

—A person who serves mankind

in ways

for which they are not grateful.

Objective

—A delusion which other lunatics share.

P

Pedant

—A man who likes his statements to be true.

R

Queer

—Basing opinions on evidence.

Rational

—Not basing opinions on evidence.

Sacrifice

—Accepting the burdens of a great position.

T

True

—What passes the examiners.

Unfair

—Advantageous to the other party.

Virtue

—Submission to the government.

Wisdom

—The opinions of our ancestors

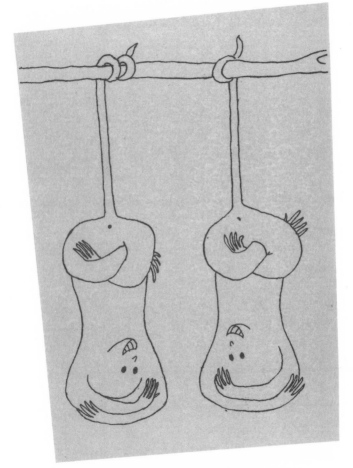

X

Xenophobia

—The Andorran opinion that the inhabitants of Andorra are the best.

Youth

—What happens to the old
when in a movement.

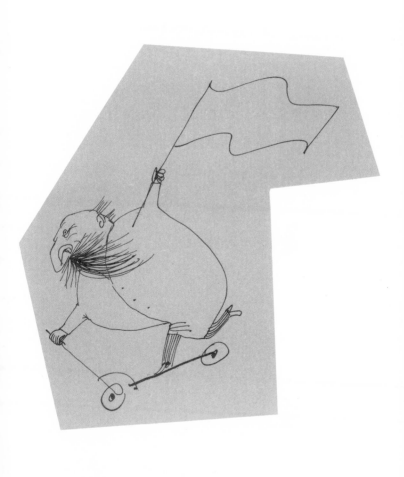

Zeal

—See stool pigeon.

Bertrand Russell

HISTORY OF THE WORLD

✳ ✳ **in epitome** ✦ ✦

{ For use in Martian infant schools }

Since Adam
and Eve ate
the apple,

man has

never

refrained

from

any

folly

of which

he was

capable

The End

Bertrand Russell
April, 1960.

THE STORY OF THIS BOOK

In 1950, Stefan Themerson sends his novel *Bayamus* to Bertrand Russell, who likes it. This marks the beginning of their correspondence and their life-long friendship. Their letters are mostly about philosophy, but also about the possibility of the Themersons' Gaberbocchus Press publishing 'Zahatapolk', Russell's story for children, with Franciszka's illustrations.

Unfortunately, Stanley Unwin (Russell's publisher at the time) objects and Russell, in an effort to alleviate the Themersons' disappointment, sends them the text for *The Good Citizen's Alphabet* as a Christmas present in 1952: 'I enclose something that has no purpose beyond fun. I can imagine delicious illustrations by Mrs Themerson.'

A few weeks later, Russell writes to say that he is 'entirely agreeable to anything you wish to do in regard to printing and date of publication and also as regards your suggestion of a de luxe edition signed by me ... You ask about terms. I had thought of making my alphabet a Christmas present, and if you are willing I should prefer to leave it so. I should not care to ask for royalties on what may well prove an unprofitable venture.'

Russell agrees to a hundred de luxe copies because that is the number he could sign. As far as the jacket blurb is concerned he wants to avoid anything 'solemn or portentous for such a very light work. Why not "P is for Pedant, who wrote this book" and then a reproduction of the picture of me with the letter P.' He sends a short list of friends to receive the author's complimentary copies, including the philosophers Rupert Crawshay-Williams and A.J. Ayer; and the artists Julian Trevelyan and Jacob Epstein.

Russell likes Franciszka's drawings, and frequently says so: 'The oftener I look at your pictures the more pleasure they give me.' He writes on 11 April 1953: 'I was charmed by the notice of the *Alphabet* in the *Observer*, but I think you ought to warn people that although P is a portrait of the author, N is not a portrait of the artist. Otherwise there is a risk that people meeting you for the first time may be disappointed!' Russell continues to take warm interest in Gaberbocchus Press, Stefan's writings and Franciszka's drawings. The publication of other stories is planned and discussed.

In April 1960, the Themersons receive from Russell a sheet of paper with six typewritten lines – the *History of the World in Epitome*. They make a little booklet with this text and Franciszka's drawings in a gold cover and send it to Russell. He likes it and asks if he may keep it.

Two years later the Themersons publish, for his 90th birthday, this booklet in a gold cover *hors commerce*, for Russell to use as he will. Later still, the *History of the World in Epitome* becomes the supplement to the Gaberbocchus paperback edition, and to this edition by Tate Publishing.

There are three Gaberbocchus editions of the book and three by other publishers, all of them include Russell's introduction.

– Bertrand Russell, *The Good Citizen's Alphabet* (first edition, 1953), Russell's captions to twenty-six letters of the alphabet illustrated by Franciszka Themerson with 28 drawings on different colour panels.

– A deluxe limited edition of 100 numbered copies was also published in 1953, each one signed by Russell and printed on hand-made paper.

– A smaller, paperback edition with black and white images was published in 1970. This edition also included Russell's 1962 *jeu d'esprit*, 'History of the World in Epitome – for use in Martian infant schools'. This 14-page supplement with two drawings by Franciszka Themerson and a photograph of an atomic explosion, was originally published *hors commerce* in a golden paper cover, to celebrate Russell's 90th birthday on 18th May 1962.

– An edition by The Wisdom Library, A Division of Philosophical Library, New York was published in 1958.

– An Italian edition (translated by Simone Barillari), *L'alfabeto del buon cittadine e Compendio di storia del mondo*, was published in 2007 by Nutrimenti, Rome.

– A French edition (translated by Lionel Menasché), *L'Alphabet du bon citoyen*, was published in 2011 by Éditions Allia, Paris.

Jasia Reichardt

This edition published 2017 by order of the Tate Trustees
by Tate Publishing, a division of Tate Enterprises Ltd,
Millbank, London SW1 4RG
www.tate.org.uk/publishing

A catalogue record for this book is available from the
British Library

ISBN 978 1 84976 530 5
Reproduction by DL Imaging, London
Printed in and bound in China